The ∾ Badass Brontës

Jane Satterfield

First Edition 2023 © Jane Satterfield
All rights reserved.
ISBN: 978-1-939728-57-9
Printed in Honesdale, Pennsylvania
Cover image by Kelly Louise Judd, *Sinking In*

Diode Editions is an independent press based in Doha, Qatar and Richmond, Virginia. Editor in Chief Patty Paine founded the press in 2012 as an offshoot of Diode Poetry Journal.

Our mission is to beautifully craft our books, and to fanatically support our authors.

Patty Paine, **Founding Editor-in-Chief**
Law Alsobrook, **Art Director and Editor**
Zoë Shankle Donald, **Managing Editor**

Diode Editions
PO BOX 5585
Richmond, Virginia 23220-0585
www.diodeeditions.com

The Badass Brontës: Contents

§

Reading Emily Brontë by Long Island Sound

Life is short & art is all & the day is dazzling,
        a glassine surface,

the clouds a mottled counterpane. The view
        splays blue, ring-billed gulls parse the tide.

No lark or heather-bells,
        just pages where the seasons swing.

You walked away from village chatter,
        toward the waterfall's campaign,

up moorland hills where a wind beat
        a path through grass. You found license

in stolen afternoons of hidden constellations—
        the silver trail of snails, a fistful

of bees roused from sleep. Your dress was a welter
        of thunder clouds & lightning bolts—

Today I'm gauze & flutter sleeves. Would you
        say the here & now is a horizon

to eternity? An ancient ice-sheet engineered
        this estuary & the sheltered

tide that slows the pulse is one mercy
        in a warming season.

I

"Some one speaking of [Emily Brontë] to me, in a careless kind of strength of expression, said 'she never showed regard to any human creature; all her love was reserved for animals.' The helplessness of an animal was its passport to Charlotte's heart; the fierce, wild, intractability of its nature was what often recommended it to Emily."

—Elizabeth Gaskell
The Life of Charlotte Brontë

"Why ask to know the date—the clime?
More than mere words they cannot be..."

—Emily Brontë
Untitled poem, September 14, 1846

Letter to Emily Brontë

Remembering Staffordshire, 1994

I'm writing this from lockdown on a day
when the dogwood throws out its dose
of darker pink. The schoolyard
across the street is wreathed in yellow
caution tape. I'm weighing uncertain
evidence on vectors & runners' strides—
what practiced motion keeps us safe, what
physics of distancing? Emily, you were no stranger
to contagion in a town of trash heaps & overflowing
pits. A *fog-bound pestilence* vapored through
low-lying towns, typhus & TB ravaged
boarding schools where pedagogues punished
the body to instruct the soul. You watched
your mother's swift decline, composed
a stoic soul. Once I lived within
a few miles of those heathered moors
where you worked out plots that swirled
around the heart's tenancy. I remember
high, cold clouds, the wind wild
at Withens. Today I practiced patience,
tipping teaspoonsful of beaten egg into batter.
Of my word count, I'm not proud.
Vaquita, Sumatran rhino, Clarion Island wren
are on the verge of vanishing & from our tiny
windows on the world, who wouldn't wish to be
each image of rewilding—dolphins freewheeling
in the absent wakes of vaporetti, herds
surging former squares of commerce—no matter
if some of the stories are spliced
from other seasons & settings. Emily,
you held onto hardiness, walked & walked
in whatever weather. A woman who could
self-cauterize a sheepdog's bite knows
fire as good medicine. Dithering makes
the mind a desert. I could use your audacity,
the refuge of a stubborn vision.

Becoming a Brontë

Patrick Brunty or Prunty was born in County Down, Ireland, and adapted the spelling of his surname while a student of St. John's College, Cambridge.

Emily, where did you get your name?
        It's said your family roots are shallow,
scant transplants to the Yorkshire moors
        where wind warps tenacious trees.

A name is both a styling and a spell
        through time's tidal sweep,
your name a lifeline to some legendary clan
        of Ulster scribes whose songs

carved out a far horizon's histories.
        O'Pronntaigh—an incantation,
bestowal or monastic space—
        Bruntee, Prunty, Brunty, each offshoot

further away from the Gaelic root.
        The right name could elevate
a scholar's origins, sever links to an unloved homeland,
        signal loyalty to the Crown.

Which impulse struck him on that day
        your father strode through pastureland
as cattle grazed near the Cam—
        apprentice poet distracted by skies

the color of tarnished coins, dreaming
        of a perpetual curacy?
Watch him sign
        the College register, wrist flowing

with a flourish, reborn as *Brontë*
        in this instant, channeling
the ancient Greek: as dynamic and ineradicable
        as thunder.

"Made Alive in the Usual Manner": Pillar Portrait of the Brontë Sisters, ca. 1834

After The Brontë Sisters (Anne Brontë; Emily Brontë; Charlotte Brontë),
by Patrick Branwell Brontë, oil on canvas, ca. 1834

Picture the household—shambolic—though they've
composed themselves into patient sitters, settling

on a pose, holding the pose, brother bantering
while he works, brush to palette, canvas, jar...
Spent colors drift like clouds reflected in a stream,

remnants of heady days when they played gods
bringing back the dead in kingdoms besieged

by revolutionaries, renegades, and rakes.
The Twelves—toy soldiers that sparked

sibling scribblemania—now molder in a tin.
Their household's shambolic. This picture's

a poor remnant. Heady days? They played. Were gods
turning squabbles into sagas. Now the sisters cling
to tomboy boots, practice showy accomplishments.

His "Battel Book" is tucked away; politics and more will
pull him from his sisters' sphere, a slow and spectral vanishing.

Hunger Strike, Haworth, Yorkshire, ca. 1836

Emily Brontë presents an ultimatum to Aunt Branwell.

All day I've stoked the kitchen fires, plumbed
the healing texts, made tinctures, teas

while Tabby rests her wounded leg, a busted mess
of bone. Having slipped on ice, she worried most

about doing damage—the post she dropped,
our brother's outgoing letters scattered. And now

you want to send her packing, wageless, back
to her sister's home because nursing an invalid

is costly, her backlog of labor now our own?
Dear Aunt, maternal sister who stepped in after

our mother died, Papa's right hand all these years,
your lodestars are duty, generosity. You've shared

the gift of your purse and time, our days disciplined
by your edicts: long walks and lessons that schooled us

toward a more harmonious key.
It's true you indulged us, too—sometimes

our childish games got wild—but more
than cake or currant buns, for more years than you care

to credit, Tabby's stories fed our hunger—
local gossip, the fairy folk whose doings

occur just out of view. Have you left
the kingdom of the benevolent? Today, we sisters

stand agreed: this injury is a call to action.
Do you worry we can't keep pace with Tabby's

rota of kitchen work? Aunt,
we have perfected pie, and the seams we've sewed

contain cartographies. What good are girls
who mince their words? Without Tabby among us,

no morsel will please. Let the table sway
with steaming broth, turnips, mutton,

rounds of bread: we'll have none until/unless she stays,
set up and salubrious, queened in this motherless lair.

Self-Portrait as Thunder and Lightning

> *Apparently, Emily did have a dress that had a thunder and lightning pattern on it,*
> *which is amazing. It's sort of telling of her character.*
>
> —Chloe Pirrie

She stabs at stitchery, affecting a fix with fine tucks.
Thrift makes a fine muse.

A house is sometimes a prison, sometimes a palace.
Fold a linen and out flies a wish.

The fabric for patience is fluid. The set task—sitting still.
An apron is coarse courage: egg splash, a welter of stains.

The romantic sister believes elaborate smocking honors Creation.
The faithful one admits to adornment's sorcery.

The corseted body is morally firm; the pretty heroine, artless.
Tight-lacers are rarely tempted to stray.

A new wife's ease with her "duties" is signaled by her light-colored summer dress.
A ripping good yarn dresses up social critique.

Daydreams may induce a distempered mind.
Literature cannot be the business of women, and it ought not to be...

When sisters style themselves as men, they stride in hunters' jackets and kilts.
Updrafts caressing the thigh, a laughable huff on cigars.

The romantic sister's dress will survive, time-tanked in museum glass.
Admirers will flash by in leggings branded *Look at Me Now!*

Far from the whirl of woolen mills, thunder and lightning
walk, indifferent to fashion's flattery, the tyranny of trends,

quicksilver in the eyes of the fox,
in the flare and flame of the fox threading high hills with its ochre.

Emily's Apocrypha

Wafting across the moors in a cloud of Yorkshire mist, the so-called sphinx of English literature has acquired almost supernatural status. The absences surrounding her have made her all the more magnetic and some colourful apocrypha has emerged to fill the gaps.

—Lucasta Miller

did not include the dour black plumage
of today's lashing rain, though the hills
in her time and town would have rung

with a similar hammering sound,
worsening wind erasing horizons
and heather. Did not include the whirl

of sirens, though maybe she'd have heard
the purring cat curled up to the grating's
edge while embers alternately flared

and cooled. Moor walker and maybe
mystic who knew a book might be an index
of birds, maybe amid a brother's intemperate

rage, Emily watched a spider cross the flagstone
floor, ink-thick in its advance, retreat;
reckoned that a pistol's kickback

is nothing next to the heart's: torqued
muscle pumping its own fugue.
Linnet, skylark, curlew, cuckoo; lapwing

with rainbow feathers and furling crest,
merlin of the steel grey eye—
She *did* know the world of tearing talons,

poacher's traps, what cruelty in man
begets. Sometimes, she spoke too frankly
but mostly held her tongue, tired out at teas,

with social calls. Village paths gave or didn't
beneath those scruffy boots.
She was no small-town sibyl, stitching

stuttered measures from some divine source.
Nor did she die on an ebony horsehair-filled couch
several inches short of her lanky height.

If good sense demanded a fire iron
across her arm to seal a sheepdog's bite,
she wore its flaming sigil, and if a spray

of flour hung in the kitchen's heat,
it shone as moments, marginalia, scrawled
notes stashed in a locked desk box,

her mastiff crouched nearby,
becalmed though still a beast,
held at bay like a devouring flame.

Animalia

—lost the Hawk Nero which with the geese was given away
and is doubtless dead for when I came back from Brussels
I enquired on all hands and could hear nothing of him—
—Emily Brontë, diary paper, Thursday, July 30, 1845

I am done for now with the day's damage
of spilled ink & little headspace,

my sisters' jests that writing pulls me away
whenever there's bread to be made,

but should this be my reward after a year abroad—
This empty cage, & family evasions? They know

I've long felt most at home in the kingdom animalia,
struck by plumage, bite & bate, alloys of fur

& flickering eyes. Call me smitten or elusive,
inspecting herbs while geese honk at my heels,

the merlin Nero upon my glove, snapping
at choicest cuts of beef. Chide me for avoiding callers,

cordials, cake, & the smallest talk, but I've suffered
through morning toast & tea, endured the garrison

of complaints: the mess, the noise, work made by
my absence, how the birds ran wild or hung about.

For "lost," I read "turned loose"; from the lack
of convincing reports, a quiet conspiracy to rob me

of beloved companions. Neighbors hesitate,
Father keeps busy, sisters suddenly hold their tongues,

but I've seen how the heath will offer up
its savage storms. The heart must be the same—

strangely arrayed, unstrung as any wind-stripped skeleton
below a raptor runaway shooed into early frost.

The Sharp-Shinned Hawk

is tiny, long-tailed, works
by stealth in all seasons,
conducting aerial dives

from perches in foliage,
scattering feathers of
songbirds in its path.

It can soar to great heights
or fly low to the ground
to take out its prey,

circling out in the open
with its flap-&-glide
flight. No longer endangered,

it has rebounded, one bright strand
in the story of time &
vanishing. My window opens

onto unseasonable weather—
no frost wreathing the glass—
above the clatter of traffic

where a lone raptor rides
the high currents, only
to slip out of sight.

At breakfast, Emily fed
bits of bacon & beef to
the merlin she rescued. The heart,

like the sharp-shinned hawk,
is trainable, if a little
high strung. Consider its range

of alarm calls & chatter.

Gigan for a Pandemic Winter

[The Brontës] were quite literally writing at the source of global industrial society.
—Terry Eagleton

For the Brontës, 'nature' was in flux—already fragile, hybrid, and compromised...
—Shawna Ross

I walked, all winter, what's mine of wilderness—
the silent fields held down by fescue, crab grass,

clover. While others tracked the numbers, kept
the count, I walked beyond the shuttered school,
in, around and through a stand of ash, elm,

and upland oak that formed a broken canopy.
Some days the sky worked its monochromatic magic,

grey or blue, to elevate a mood. Sometimes a raptor
rose and fell, sliding between centuries, to where

we had not yet coined the word *anthropocene*.
I walked. What's mine of wilderness?

The broken canopy of days? The field was edged
with snow, then snowdrops, sparklers, cans of
Twisted Tea. Once three sisters watched the world

turn its direction, wrote through geographies of grief.
That shattered silence—a glove thrown on the ground.

Emily Brontë's Advice for the Anthropocene

Hers is a Green and animal beyond...
—Stevie Davies, *Emily Brontë: Heretic*

Haworth was a maze
of multiplying middens, mills, the pumped-up
clouds of industry, heathered moors a haven in
a century's shrinking space. Tempting, yes,
to stick to chores, scrub the parlour carpet,
remain, in fact, remote. But as the saying goes,
there is no later. This is later—arctic ice melts,
shears off; strange calvings stun the circumspect
to speech. If Emily were here today,
what would she say? Though twilight calls
for a generous pour, it's better to learn dark
sonatas, the heart's own haul of grief.
The soul's compass is—or ought to be—
set straight for the storm. Some species
die without a fellow creature's comfort—
sparrows sometimes fail to thrive when solitary.
The auk's line, I've read, unraveled when stumblers
dropped the eggs. Troubadours enshrine
the human truths—lies, betrayals, love
gone astray. What else would she tell us?
Aim to take dictation—a rabbit
grooming in the grass calls down the watchful hawk,
the robin's clutch in turn attracts the foraging crow.
And would we listen to her counsel
as we stand stoic in the bracing air, embrace
the static stare of endlings? *Look up*, she'd say,
you will come to call them kin.

II

"Modern depictions of the Brontës become interesting when they reveal a dimension of the Brontës in a new way, even while departing from the truth in order to do so."

—Abigail Burnham Bloom
"The Brontë Family in Popular Culture" in
A Companion to the Brontës (Blackwell, 2016)

"They are beloved by everyone from misunderstood teens and fools for love to the serious-minded middle aged and those of a critical bent. Now the Brontës are taking centre stage again…"

—Sarah Hughes
"Why those subversive Brontë sisters still hypnotise us," *The Guardian*, March 26, 2016

§

"Well, some may hate and some may scorn.
And some may quite forget thy name…"

—Emily Brontë, "Stanzas to –"
poem dated November 14, 1839

The Badass Brontës

are up to here with aunt's old-time religion,
their brother's boozy brawls. They'll walk miles
in unhip boots, unfazed by hail or funnel clouds,
slinging sweet iambics to help them keep the pace.
Anne's irked past words with nannying and given in
her notice—good riddance to the coked-up
financier and his straying wife, the schoolboy
stoning sparrows, the chronic cleaning up.
She's breathing freer now a Gothic cross heaves
between her breasts. Some nights she leads
kitchen karaoke, is not above canoodling
in the crypts with her father's curate. Charlotte downs
a dirty chai to plot another romance novel.
She'll lock the doors and justify her genius,
rifling through her sisters' desks. She's no ordinary
busybody, "just looking for a pen." Her love letters
to her old prof are full of pretty filthy stuff—
submissive dreams and words like whips. Emily's
an insomniac, works from dusk 'til dawn and still
finds time for pistol practice—survivalism calls.
When hailed to play piano, she'll unleash a dark
fugue on unwitting guests and call her hawk
down with a whistle—watch out, she'll throw
red wine in your face. Beguiling cocktails?
They can't even. Their laughter sets the house
abuzz as any hive. They go commando when
they can, in town or on the primrose path.

Which Brontë Sister Are You?

Suggested by Internet quizzes that align your answers with one of the sisters' profiles

You're just like *Emily*, quiet and courageous —
You don't need any man to speak for you.
What secrets are you holding? Let them guess —
like Emily, you're quietly courageous,
unfazed by ghosts or storms, mysterious...
Your eye is drawn to creatures deemed past rescue.
A free spirit in a vintage dress, you burn, courageous,
untouched by any man who speaks to you.

§

Your plainness can't disguise that you're ambitious.
Like duty-bound *Charlotte*, hoping for romance,
the rakes you can't reform prove you're rebellious.
You can't disguise your pain. Still, you're ambitious
to pen a stellar tale against officious
men who envy your prose and cash advance...
It's plain. You can't disguise it. You're ambitious,
despite your façade of duty, hope, romance.

§

Sidelined by show-offs, you're gentle with a steely core.
You're reserved, like *Anne*, intelligent and reflective.
You live your life as if touched by a higher power —
Your pen is a weapon. You're steely at the core —
Confronting the injustice you deplore,
you fight to the bitter end. And you forgive
your show-off siblings, though you do keep score —
however reserved, well-mannered, and reflective.

The Brothers Bell Plead Publishers Not to be Unmasked

The enigma of the Brothers Bell is not worth solving...
—Charlotte Brontë

Certainly it injures no one else for us to remain quiet, to publish separately or together—rumors swirl around our identities—*Who is Ellis? Who is Currer? Who is Acton?* Are we brothers of the weaving order in some Lancashire town? A single voice peddling sordid tales? Are the novels that we pen mere patchwork—one chapter the work of a Miss or Missus; the next born of a husband's guiding hand, an editor's sure & manly vision? If women, then radical, surely unsexed...

Acton is neither Currer nor Ellis—we are distinct & unconnected...black-jacketed, fob-watched, purchasing our quires of paper, fair narrators suspected of schemes, of fictitious signatures. Few would dispute that novels are meant for both men & women to read. Strange that authoresses are looked on with prejudice, fancied as frivolous, faced with a crooked ratio of word to coin?

—& what of ambition throttled by purveyors of propriety? Authors upended by citizen critics, beset by a curate here, a pious and parochial merchant there?

Forget the notion of a unified firm! We are three, each resolved to preserve our incognito, our duty to speak unpalatable truths. We do not write with a view of celebrity, a love of sensation. Masked, we pace the village in peace, amble the far fields, feral in freedom...We know whose business literature is. Before the public we must be gentlemen. Imagine us bantering into the night & by the fireside, ferocious—Ellis in his easy chair drawing, Acton sewing—a rash act.

Costumery: Cento with Lines from Early Reviews of *Wuthering Heights*

*Charlotte, Emily, and Anne Brontë posed as Currer, Ellis, and Acton Bell to
publish their work; rumors swirled around the nature of their identity and their
novels' composition.*

The whole firm of Bell & Co.
              staring down human life—

A depravity strangely their own
              One family, one pen—

Provincialisms, blasphemy, the brutalizing influence
              of unchecked passion—

Scenes so hot, emphatic
              so sternly masculine in feeling—

Its sex cannot be mistaken
              even in manliest attire—

A sprawling story casts a gloom
              One presiding evil genius—

Two generations of sufferers
              The highest effects of the supernatural—

An atmosphere of mist
              A more natural unnatural story

we do not remember having read
              but what may be the moral?

Tempers spoiled in childhood
              violence, dogged obstinacy—

A ferocity fatal to tranquility
              Rakes and battered profligates—

Nightmares and dreams, many chapters
              Good dashes of character, too—

But however well these Brothers Bell
        may write by rule and line

their work still bears the stamp of more
        than one mind and one sex

sundry guises, sundry authors
        What we may call costumery

Emily, Inked

Imagining tattoos for Emily

She loves hidden histories,
        windows to other worlds—

the darts & daggers,
        hearts & arrows—

the transported's memoirs, marks
        & signatures

fashioned en route
        to Van Diemen's Land—.

The floral bracelets
        London women

etched on wrists, an improvised
        low-cost jewelry...

She loves the juxtaposition of design,
        skin devotional

with decoration, porous
        as a page—

Keeper in the kitchen,
        Nero in his cage,

Victoria & Adelaide
        (the geese that got away).

Whinchat, ring ousel,
        a double-stumped

wind-gnarled fir tree,
        stars clustered

in sisterly constellation.
        A hawk kiting,

wings unfurled, holding
   its position in the air.

A fox kit sunning by a cairn,
   bluebells banded in a ring.

Errant notes & sharps
   reined in by a stave,

a hedgehog, all inky spined...
   An errant queen's knotted brooch.

The frost & fire of Gondal's glittering
   geography, high waving

heather—a girl, her brother fleeing
   from the palaces of instruction.

The Misses Brontës' Establishment

> *...we were thinking of setting up a school—the scheme has been dropt and long after*
> *taken up again and dropt again because we could not get pupils—...*
> —Anne Brontë, diary paper, Thurs., July 31, 1845

Our school offers board & education to a limited
number of young ladies training

for life in the *private sphere*. Safely installed
with well-qualified sisters,

you'll cultivate needed accomplishments
& enjoy the use of a pianoforte. Success

for a woman relies on a balance
of headwork & housekeeping—it's not enough

to sew straight seams from here to tomorrow.

§

For those who need to earn their way,
we're here with other lessons. Keep your work-box

in good order! No matter how angry, a governess will learn
to bite delicately into blancmange, to dispatch a letter

with charm. Expect that your charges will mount
daily mutinies.
                    A teacher must be

the very definition of docile & have on hand
whatever she needs in the event

of landslide or armed insurrection.

§

Art offers advantages, too—painters
& illustrators work remotely, their privilege & luck

to labor at home, secure in the joys
of domestic life.
                    Writing offers a similar advantage,

but women authors must remain blameless—
The reading public tends to confuse unmannerly characters

with their creator.

                    §

Of course arithmetic/history/grammar/geography
help any woman manage a home, nor does

learning have to preclude the building up
of a hot trousseau. When you leave

the unmarried state, assume you'll endure all forms of love.
Conduct manuals offer limited guidance—you'll glean

much more from novels & gossip, your position
assured once you snuff the guttering candles,

secure in your splendid talents.

                    §

Finally, the pupils of our establishment
are promised the usual comforts—one pillowcase,

a set of sheets, four towels, dessert & tea spoons.
You'll be encouraged to botanize

when walking out or taking the air, noting both flora & fauna
as you follow the fox's trail, the arc

& dive of the local hawk.
                              But steer clear of the poisoned well,
the districts that no young lady enters, the crags

embroidered with moss from which the descent is steep.

Errand Hanging with Emily Brontë

> Emily Brontë's Shopping Trolley, *drawing by Conrad Atkinson, 2009, coloured pencil, watercolour, printing, and acrylic paint on paper*

Let's admit it's good to get out
in streets no longer emptied
by plague. That we're over winter,
the camo leggings of quarantine
fashion. I'll take Emily at her word: of ways
to be ordinary, this might be
fun—pushing trolleys with uncertain
finesse past fitness gurus gathering
cacao nibs & community-traded
tea. I could use a sister to interrogate
my knowledge of toxins & need
for another pair of super-soft jeans. Watch me
lean in when the gossip gets good—her brother's
negligence in keeping accounts, the neighbors'
Twitter feuds, the family still fuming
over her brief flirtation with Occupy.
No one would call her queasy. Still,
she'll query the butcher about
the origins of the Irish salmon,
the dry-rubbed baby back ribs.
She's writing songs now—do I think
the vocals could use more reverb? Smoky cocktails
& sliding cheeseboards are delightful
distractions, if not promising cures.
She'd say a trolley (from dialect, *low cart
with flanged wheels*) is a proper shiny
conveyance good for gathering books
& greens, though I notice linnets & butterflies
are already flying free of its bars.
The aesthetics of business are ugly but
Emily makes short work of the weekly shop.
Farewell, green ivy, feathered fern,
fall leaf. At the farmer's market, we'll admire
the varietals— Sungold, Apero, Gardener's
Delight— & how they signal a lateral move
through harvest, forage, & feast. She'll toast
our pact to ditch doomsday novels, swap

stress-relief jewelry for time in the dirt, hands
upturning earth's microbiome for health.
Let's admit we all could use a companion
in times of vanishing seasons.

Own the Charlotte Brontë

*A single-family home model available in two communities in Maryland
from Ryan Homes*

In the midst of McMansions, a dream of enchantment—
live like a Brontë
but with all the extras beyond reach of a clerical family.

Call up the memory of peaceful days, of English
countryside cottages
minus the cruel wind, moorland damp, and factory smoke.

Imagine rooms brimming with light, gracious columns
that bolster the entry.
Why not curate your space with herbal arrangements, personal crafts?

(It's less tedious than putting out fires accidentally lit
by a beer-addled brother. . .)
The butler's pantry offers plenty of space for stashing

extra maker supplies. What won't you do with reclaimed wood,
repurposed materials?
Maybe fashion the sort of work box a governess would have used

to store *oceans of needlework, yards of cambric to hem?* (Good thing
you don't have to live on her salary. . .)
Rest easy, there's ample space for a garden, safe haven

from chaos and climate change. As for plumbing, the mud and miasmas
that burdened this model's namesake
are nothing to fear today. Use a quiet nook as your study—

you can scribble into the night under electric candlelight
or live out a real-life romance—
Just think of your fun when the cloaks come off, good times

stretched out in the soaking tub, away from the village
and prying eyes. Don't fret!
You're far enough from the flood plain to let all worries tumble away.

You can stock up on ink and stationer's stock (the sustainable kind,
of course), and as any
unreformed rake is likely to say, Trust us—you'll be wowed.

The Most *Wuthering Heights* Day Ever

> *An annual gathering held in various locations across the globe since*
> *2016; participants recreate the music video of Kate Bush's 1978 hit*
> *song "Wuthering Heights."*

You love it wild—the wind & weather,
red lipstick perfect for a new romance—
Today will be the most *Wuthering Heights* Day ever.

You've seen the Kate Bush video: voice aquiver,
she sings "Wuthering Heights" half in a trance—
red Cathy dress rippling in the wind & weather.

With green eye shadow you'll conjure moors & heather.
Gals, grannies, bearded blokes will synchronize in dance—
Will today be their most "Wuthering Heights" Day ever?

Some love the song but not the book—whatever!
To Emily, local gossip & happenstance
would yield her novel's whirl of wind & weather,

though scholars wonder, "Did she have a lover?"
Three hundred Cathys attract more than a glance,
moves choreographed: the most "Wuthering Heights" Day ever.

From Dublin to Tel Aviv, fans catch the fever—
cellphones capturing flash mobs as they twirl, advance,
& love it, wildly—the wind & weather
synced for the most *Wuthering Heights* Day ever.

Who is Heathcliff?

Wuthering Heights *is the perfect example of how the traces of slavery are not new news and can be found in seemingly unusual sources.*
—Susan Gillman "Remembering Slavery, Again,"
Los Angeles Review of Books, February 7, 2016

...if Heathcliff was not a black African or descendant of one, historians have comprehensively demonstrated that he very easily might have been...Emily Brontë was aware of local debates about abolition and she knew about the impact of sugar wealth on her neighbourhood through a host of personal associations.
—Corinne Fowler, "Was Emily Brontë's Heathcliff black?"
Think: Leicester Arts, Society and Culture, October 25, 2017

A foundling,   an orphan,

    a source of debate.

A castaway from Liverpool streets

    or deckhand from a colonial ship—

Of what country, what race?

    Can anyone know?

Banished to fields

    by a cruel foster brother.

Three years with no record—

    a narrative gap...

What profit or plunder is agent or source

    of the fortune he earned

after fleeing the Heights?

    The orphan transformed

to a country squire—

    heathen & husband, hanger of dogs.

From the ashy hearth of his home arisen

    a misanthrope's heaven

of stone-guarded gloom.

He grew in the wellspring

      of violence & learned

his unbending love

      for a woman constrained,

no longer *half-savage hardy and free*

      kept from roaming

the thunderstruck moors...

      Black eyed, furrowed brow,

a landlord who learned

      that a tyrant should crush

all within reach.

      A *dark thing* driving his love to the grave.

The outsider who learned *godless indifference*

      from the movements of merchants,

the amnesia of custom,

      from the circuits of ships,

the clatter of coins...

      Broken souls broken bodies...

In the pallor of parlors,

      Caribbean sugar,   chocolate and tea,

Imported coffee,   Virginia Tobacco,

      American cotton,

      mahogany—

that tropical wood which holds the hue

      of suffering hands

in a master's house.

Heathcliff's Curse

After learning that his beloved Catherine has married his rival Edgar Linton,
Heathcliff speaks his wish for vengeance.

Let legions of thorn
        tangle eaves

& ivy darken windows.
        Let clouds

begin to script a storm. I call
        on all avenging spirits—

Unmake the magnates
        of industry, the makers

of mills, breakers
        of will. I've watched love

waste *in the soil of shallow*
        cares, a woman wilt

in rooms of vases,
        values, her body burning

for open space...Forget songsters &
        caged birds—call down

the carrion-seekers. Let one
        bird of bad omen

enter the nest, uproot
        the scrabbling brood.

I've seen the way that dice
        take a turn, coins

thicken a foundling's purse.
        As the gorse inherits

the hills, hunkers its roots'
        indelible lines—

This curse I bring upon myself,
        banished from your gaze,

as the murdered haunts
        the murderer, as long

as I am living—heed me,
        haunt me, rise

into unrest, ghost my heart's
        tenantless realm.

Spellcasters

...[T]here's something almost mythical about the Brontë creation story, the idea of these three isolated young women writing so desperately that the words were almost flung on to the page. Ted Hughes called them the "three weird sisters", intentionally summoning Macbeth's blasted heath to Haworth parsonage.
    —Sarah Hughes, "Why those subversive Brontë sisters still
    hypnotise us," *The Guardian*, March 26, 2016

I'll show you how far I've progressed in the Black Art—
    —Catherine Earnshaw, on being accused of practicing witchcraft
    by the servant Joseph in *Wuthering Heights*

Weird, you say? Well, fair enough—
seeing how we're sat, hellbent
at books & candle-lit. Nocturnal
truth: we sweep aside polished
cutlery, cooled remnants
of the feast, circling round
the family table to conjure
gothic plots, sometimes walking
widdershins & weird is
striding out by day?— a steady pace
past all things mechanical, the church
bells marking time & clattering
of textile mills that drove
the fairy folk away. No secret
that we're no one's darlings,
just the curate's girls whose bit
of brogue to village ears seems
a heathen tongue. If jumping
stiles is weird, we'll take it—tired
of seams & taming, watch us curl
into a snooze with foxes, wake up
mouthy & magnificent. Our habitation's
where the air's grown thin & walls
between worlds weaken, poised
beneath the high stones'
shadows where the atmosphere
is sizzling & supercharged. We grew up
tossing elf-bolts, watched them skim
the surface of the stream, muslin dresses

hiked thigh-high as we shimmied
up the rock face. Weird is marshalling
the high, cold clouds, mastering
all aspects of moonlight & mist,
charms that tear the veil of domesticity—
here's heather Charlotte plucked at summer's
height; for wealth & weal, a potent
crumb, a disused spider web. For love,
Anne, would you advise rose quartz
as steady flame? When the east
wind turns malevolent, salt lays down
a protective circle, & I banish bad luck
with a bulb planted in a page's ash.
From the land we draw the bond of blood
that was our mother's benediction & call
on all the green ones to bless all those
who fight for crusts. We call on air &
fire, water, earth & spirit: let them lift
toxins from the well, plump up drying
peat, rule the rain to stay the floods &
heal the anchoring hedges. May they
roll back the besmirching smoke
that the ancient forest might rise again,
more real than Birnam wood. Bring back
sweet chestnut, beech, & red oak, rich
soil & verdant canopies, lemon slug,
purple emperor, wood anemone.
We ask benevolence for the bees,
the gift of summer in a jar. What good
are words if they don't weave a web
that spans the centuries to summon
a sisterhood of destiny? Let them walk
the rugged earth & know we have arrived.

III

"... *Jane Eyre* and *Wuthering Heights* are not things to be forgotten. The work of Currer Bell is a great performance; that of Ellis Bell is only a promise, but it is a colossal one."

—Anonymous, *Atlas*, January 22, 1848 (one of five reviews found in Emily Brontë's desk after she died)

§

"The wild deer browse above her breast;
The wild birds raise their brood..."

—Emily Brontë, "Song"
poem, dated May 1, 1844

Autobiographia Literaria

Upper Marlboro, Maryland ca. 1971 and Haworth, Yorkshire, 1830's

It's summer in Baltimore's
muscular heat & the whoosh
of a circular fan in the study

brings back a dust-scent
of books & quiet, the library
tucked in a strip mall storefront,

the children's book room
my place & escape. One
child among many, I practiced

printing my name so small, it fit
the framed box of the borrower's form.
Completed, the task earned me the right

to compile a stack of my own,
the max set at six for a week.
Truth sometimes sounds like a plot—

Imagine Emily & Anne, arms linked
while they walked several miles &
back across sodden moors

up the long, tree-lined drive
to the grey stone manor hall owned by
a kindly family who'd lend weekly newspapers

& poetry books from a library
brimming with legal volumes, Gothic romances,
even the First Folio. Imagine Charlotte,

far from home—a governess
barred from the master's shelves,
the books reserved for his use alone, though

she's charged with guiding his heirs.
A child, I dared stray no farther
from home on my own than the blackberry

bramble that ended our road...Laid down
in black ink, the librarian's stamp
marked the call for closing time. Tacked

on the wall behind her head, seascapes,
pyramids, a banner inscribed
with a woman's words: *No frigate*

like a book to take you far away.

Volumes

You should be very thankful that books cannot "talk to each other as well as to their readers." Conceive the state of your warehouse if such were the case....Terrible too would be the quarrelling... such a whispering may be heard—by those who have ears to hear.

—Charlotte Brontë to George Smith, September 18, 1850

Certain mornings you can catch the sound
        of voices as they rise and fall,
fleeting as the atmospheric scent
        of dampened wool, the strange sillage
of matted fur—faint suggestions
        of spirits unconfined by custom
and voices straying beyond their covers,
        considered whispers that reveal
metaphors and mysteries,
        baubles and confections, steps
to make a proper pie, sea charts
        and coordinates which might set the soul
on or off a righteous path...Bunyan and Boethius
        holding forth on prayer, Scott and Hoffman
on the spectral, Aesop, Coleridge and Clare
        in debate about the natural
world...A book's an invitation,
        excoriation, sustenance, pilgrimage
or vice, a tangled web of inscriptions
        that maps its own cartography...Oracular
or otherwise, a book instructs, offers
        escape, has toxic side-effects which means
it must be kept in or out of hands...Certain
        mornings you can catch
the rousing chorus as authors
        parley/conspire/announce/advise—
folly, fancy, wit and wisdom
        within the *lettered leaves*—
Byron at odds with Bewick, speeches
        that end with a flourish, celebrating
passion or ennui.

Forfeit

Emily returns to the memory of her lost hawk, Nero

I know a hawk from a handsaw & when Nero
came crashing down from what wound, what wonder—

I know a hawk—& the wind running armies
over grasses, hedge & path, the sky unfurled

over a fever of fields, torn petals ferried
on the stream—a hawk, handsome-feathered, rescue-won.

—I know a bite from a beak & when the wanton
spirit rises nothing mournful opens—a day's walk,

the weather fine, sunshine floating free, bog & bracken,
heather lit from within. I know hilltop, heath & stunted

firs. Thought silt & crow flowers, rue. Thought &
thought again. *A proper letter I have never performed.*

There must be magic in my taming—cuffs & collars:
the falls are fresh in mind. The hawk's wing-beat's rapid,

can't connive a cage. When clipped, is stripped of dive
& plummet, grip & tear; heart feathered, fettered. Stutter

or hop-to-hand. I thought of rumors, a remembered
sketch, the talon here, the moment tamed. Sift the embers,

scratch the meal; *I am seldom troubled with nothing
to do.* I have no answers for extreme weather, a failing

source of light. We are at home & likely to be. Or
walking out, I guess, if all goes well, toward the maw

of time. I have no answers but I knew him—quick-witted
as questions in margins, as window-clatter when the clouds

turn cool as iron, ashed in the afternoon. For a while,
a page's torn beauty—I could not countenance a flame.

Haworth of Other Days

The Brontë Parsonage Museum, 1994

The village had, that winter afternoon, the intricacy of solitude—
few walked the ice-slick streets that slope
toward the bus station and heritage train. Peat smoke
scrolled from chimneys offering its taste of boggy after-tang.

The snow that drifted down the dales
dropped like tattered lace. Beneath
the day's procession, robin, mistle-thrush, redwing;
mosses and heather like anchorites in place.

The Parsonage held out a fugue of hardly vanished voices...

Three sisters, resonant against the dark, gathered
at the drop-leaf table scarred with candle-burn and the one lone letter
floating free, a carved "E"— in Emily's hand or an afterthought
affixed years past the time her pages were set in type?
The stopped clock on the landing halfway up the stairs
explicable, like the museum shop souvenirs

                                  —novels, tea-towels, busts—
stage props from a period piece
that traced geographies of grief, lady novelists who,
like Byron, were mad, bad, and dangerous to know...Their lives were brief,
though bountiful. They inhabited realms
of imagination, the cramped circumference of their domestic
space enlarged the way a real back lane leads out and upward to the waterfall...

Where is their vanished conversation, verses tuned to sidereal time?
The ghosts of fangirls and pilgrims surrounded my every step! Was it only
ninety years ago that Woolf walked here, too,
noting the suspense she felt—

                            as if approaching some long-lost friend?
Brushed with transience, the atmosphere shone in that lost winter:
tea shops with scones and floral brews, the Black Bull's
ghostly tenant swirling there, palpable as the pulled pints of Branwell bitter.

Night

...we are all in decent health—only that papa has a complaint
in his eyes and with the exception of B [brother Branwell Brontë]
who I hope will be better and do better, hereafter.

—Emily Brontë, diary paper, Thursday, July 30, 1845

When the last rays of light gutter
the front room's fire, one's thrown
back to tinder time. By day
we are not idle, plotting to counter
future debt. The cooking gives me time
to stoke my German, parse the phrases
of major & minor sonatas. Still, I
cannot do all I wish & drive away
Branwell's chronic woes: schemes
of love gone aground & too little fame
for the poems he's published. We've slept little
since the night, dense with opium & drink,
he laced his room with fire only my own
quick-thinking doused. The scorched counterpane,
I told Charlotte, was the least of it—
Each soul must stand sentinel against
its own undoing—yes, even Branwell's.
Though we hope for better, I'll mind
the lock hereafter. It may be hours
till voices spill into the alley, the Bull's guests
gone their ways, addle-browed
with unsteady carousing & our brother
loudest among them, lingering
then storming in, leaving a wake
of broken vases...
         I'll keep
watch & turn to work. The rising moon
is as good a measure as any calculating clock.
A gathering of scrap paper is spark enough,
& the words each page will hold, a path.

The Consequences of Desire/Brontë Bodies

1. Emily encounters the healing herbs, circa 1830s

Hedge witch, I teased Tabby, less servant to us than patient mother, traipsing lane & moor in a whirl of eerie tales & local gossip. I'd say, *Books hold secrets.* She'd counter, *The land holds charms. Botanize as you will, there's more you'll need to know.*

Consider first, she said, *the culinary herbs which animate a dish—some savory, some sweet. Know which ones (& when & why) a woman's ill-advised to taste them. Consider medicinals, this for pain & this other for courses missed...*

I saw what roots beneath the bracken, gathered bilberries in summer sun. What grows above reveals where soil's luxuriant or scant—the pale pink of the cuckoo flower marks where ground is damp. We pulled back bindweed, looked for yarrow bloom where the soldier beetle rests. *Next,* I laughed, *you'll have me weave a nettle dress.*

From her I learned what calms a heart, curbs a fever, brings on sleep. What acrid brew brings best results when a purge is greatly needed, what eases tension or restores the flow...

Other days she paused, as if she saw a revenant or living image of a mother wise with cures, on hand for labor & lyings-in. Tabby whispered, shawl pulled close as we neared the waterfall, *Remember which to swap or gather, which to procure quietly. These are Eve's herbs: she took no pay for her physics.*

2. Imagining her exit, Anne prepares her resignation, 1845

My employer's house is stuffed with sweetmeats & books no one but the tutor is allowed to touch. Sometimes a scone, thickly buttered, is the sum of my mistress's largesse, though I've seen what she shares with the hired men. Meanwhile, her daughter—my charge till recently—moves beyond all influence, legs wrapped around a steed all the way to Gretna Green—a high-strung heroine in marital haste.

Dalliance is a girl's undoing—she ends up penniless or marooned, left with child or seeking a hex & whatever handiwork brings it off...Every woman knows a birth might mean her own trip to the grave. Sometimes I think my sisters have spent their lives pretending they don't mourn the mother we lost, the mother I miss but don't remember...even as girls, they wrote & wrote of love & war & heroes they'd kill off then resurrect.

But what part did my own body's passage play in my mother's leaving, those months of protracted pain, her womb inflamed until the toxins clenched her heart? Surely the Divine holds out salvation for us all...I'm told a governess must swallow dreams like some ungarnished dish. I have a pen, a wish to tell the truth, duty beyond the hedge-lined rows of this tired estate. Most days I choose to dress myself with hope, my mother's dying gift—that one small string of carnelian beads with its tiny lock.

3. Assigned to bedrest with undiagnosed hyperemesis gravidarum (HG), Charlotte posts a letter to a friend, 1855

Papa feared my marriage—& maybe he was right—to a cleric like himself. My mother seems a phantom—I recall only one or two fleeting scenes. I don't want to leave behind an orphaned brood. I've loved my hours as a wife—let London & my work recede for the wild iron-bound Irish coast where we honeymooned, slow walks & raucous riding & now I'm keeping nothing down. Even weak tea tastes like fear.

Dear A., I try to imagine better days, now that I've renounced all medicine. Sometimes a woman is the conduit for a story, sometimes she's a story of her own. I thought—once—I'd let out the seams of my best silk—this appears not to be the case—

Sometimes I think of Gaskell's advice, her genius for secrets women ought to know & if you could send me something that will do good, please do.

Archival

For the sisters I never had

If you have no sisters, summon
   the spectral & bid

your farewells—boutiques,
   banks, & Irish bars,

the flashing signage
   of assorted freedoms, hotel

where you snoozed
   through the loop of news,

or trawled dreams
   where moonlight silvered

another century's
   flagstone floor & if

the present is a singular room
   wood-paneled

with sheltered lamp-light
   where fragments float

on a lined leather case,
   ink's

a stay against time
   & Emily's lines stake

the Now—
   stiles in a snow-filled field—

§

You have no sisters, so summon
   the spectral—

voices resurrected from volumes—
   remembered from parties—one's

counsel against slinky dresses,
        another bearing

painkillers & tea—
        an exhortation, of course: courage!—

Time's currents stall
        then crest. As for the song

of ruby-crowned kinglet,
        the racoon shuffling over

dead leaves in the Ramble—
        what color ink, Emily,

would you advise—Apocalypto,
        Snowflake,

Pincushion Moss,
        Iron Girder, Cold Steel?

§

Patience & Fortitude,
        time's ruinous rain—

An archive summons
        the spectral—

marble-cool
        cathedral hush,

call slips for *realia*,
        from Latin, *the real things*

the living once touched—
        a writing slope

stained with ink,
        coil-springed creatures

in manuscript margins &
        a lock of hair

secreted inside a desk box—
        desk box like a heart

carried out
        in good weather,

or tidied at night—a heart &
        what it holds

or hides—open it:
        out flies a wish—

Rewriting Emily

> *I have just read over* Wuthering Heights, *and for the first time, have obtained a clear glimpse of what are termed (and, perhaps really are) its faults.*
>> —Charlotte Brontë, "Editors' Preface to the New Edition of *Wuthering Heights*"

> *After Emily died, Charlotte took the reins and became the impresario of her posthumous reputation. Her attempts to rewrite her in fiction, criticism, and biography, and as an editor, are often as obfuscating as they are revealing.*
>> —Lucasta Miller, *The Brontë Myth*

Because, to the critics, *the Bells must appear a bad set,*
          serving up the salacious—

Because readers are hills, and hamlets must seem
          unfamiliar, even alien, to be a 'misanthrope's heaven'—

Because she was no more than *a nursling of the moors,*
          a walker and watcher in the weather's skitter and shift—

Because her mind held *a strange though somber power*
          and *I did suspect our work was not what is called 'feminine'*—

Because she adored the uncanny
          and as little as possible put down her pen—

Because the work wants sunshine, and she worked late into the night,
          setting her heart by star time—

Because it's better to wear a mask
          than admit what you've witnessed first-hand—

Because she kept herself at a distance,
          and to adore the uncanny is to make one's critics uncomfortable—

Because she stabbed at her sampler, pulling thread
          into crooked lines, and I am always undoing the tangle—

Because she fell silent in company,
          turned away invitations to tea—

Because her will was not very flexible,
          her seclusion misunderstood—

Because I propped her up in the gardens in Brussels
     and explained her manners (homesickness) away—

Because a stream might seize her attention,
     the bluebell might be a charm—

Because she sounded ungodly in the belief inspiration was her own,
     and *Heathcliff alone stands unredeemed*—

Because she wrote in almanac margins, carving kingdoms in air,
     yet scoured carpets and kneaded dough—

Because her sketches were rugged and rooted,
     her verses blocked out to resemble newsprint—

Because she was handy with pistols and hawks,
     and Keeper still cries by her bedroom door—

Because she saw this grand machine of feast and famine,
     predator and prey—

Because she watched rain unbuckle a robin's nest,
     was bold in not holding her tongue—

Because the bracken I brought in from the heath
     festers under glass, an architecture of grief—

Had she but lived, her work might have grown magnanimous,
     and because I did what I must—

Whether it is right or advisable
     to consign letters and drafts to flame

Discarded Books at Flood Tide

After Library, *a painting by Frank Moore, 1989,*
oil on canvas framed with found book assemblage

Where have we been?
The cracked-spine novels served us well
for weathering the winter or basking summers
on the beach.
            But now they are a flood,
an epic tide of cobalt, azure, indigo
washing up scenes and stories
beside lost videotapes and disks—
the archive of some new sublime
vanishing at the horizon.

Where are we now?
An empty rowboat's reached a mooring place,
bobbing on the sodden tide
under a sky whose colors we once knew
as cornflower, midnight, or blue yonder...

Where are we going?
The elements here emit
an eerie energy. Should we
take comfort in the current? Let Swift
and Austen tumble forward, talismans
for our guided journey.
                        The fire that surges
in the distance seems historical—
smoke rising from a vanquished town
that may or may not be our own.

Sestina for Hiraeth, with Titles of Plath Poems from Early 1963

Sylvia Plath visited the Brontë Parsonage Museum on September 28, 1956;
my own visit took place in December, 1994.

One thing I won't miss is freezing fog
casting feathery ice crystals in some mystic
pattern impossible to divine. (As a child
years before, I'd known England in summer, my totem
of Shakespeare sonnets held close, the weather a kindness.)
I do miss the cool hush of cathedrals, exchanging words

with strangers. The Brontë siblings imagined worlds
of explorers and warrior queens cleaving the fog
of battle. Crows gathered as Sylvia threw kindling
on the fire, her private thoughts a mystery
even to Ted, the soulmate she trusted, to him
always both lover and stranger. I remember the chilled

flagstone entry hall at Haworth, the *Child*
Ballads I bought at the market, how insects whirred
in the henges, a stand of silver birch, bonfires totemic.
The rose-wreathed tea cups, moors in fog—
for Emily, these held the power to scatter Belgium's mist,
her exile eased by memory and her sister's kindness.

Did she miss the creatures she viewed as kin—
a hawk hand-fed, two cats, a pheasant—denizens of childhood
realms. The Welsh gave us *hiraeth*, a word that's mystical,
the longing for a homeland you can't return to—no word
my Midlands-born mother knew. Cross-legged on a field wall backed by fog,
Sylvia tapped out notes on a battered Smith-Corona, a totem

from home that foretold success, Yorkshire's totemic
sheep grazing the heather. Love made the world look kindly
though wind sheared the dales at night, a coal fire fogging
up glazed windows. Sometimes I think it's childish
to mourn the places of our past; other days, I'm wordless,
trawling images that barely capture the mystique

of rock-ridden landscapes I walked in the Peaks, mystified
when asked for directions, the tickets I saved like totems
withholding their answers. Weird's not the same as *wyrd*,
that web of fate. What comes to pass isn't always a kindness
though we nurture it like our own child,
an unfolding that leads us back home through fog—

What's mystical in a home that never was? An unkindness
of ravens becomes a totem to a child
who listens for words through a landscape's fog.

Charlotte Brontë: The Séance

Harriet Beecher Stowe summons Charlotte Brontë, May 1869

Heart-shaped, the planchette shivers.
        Questions drift, a spray
of magnolia blooms. What lies
        beyond the veil?

Blinds lift and flutter; the medium
        trawls the shuttered
dark. The fiery abolitionist falls silent
        at the pencil's trek

across the page. Years from now,
        Harriet will describe
her guide's mind: serene, "no prey
        to the embellishments

of scholarship or French"—the words
        she hears ring
true. Like elixirs, messages spill forth
        from the spirit

Harriet has admired—
        Charlotte Brontë, London's
sensation and unmasked authoress,
        another so-called "little woman"

whose ink propels resistance
        to institutions that enslave,
exposing masters who see a world
        of women, men, and children

to be crushed. The manacles
        of mind and flesh
are, to some reviewers, coarse details
        that mar fine prose,

better swept away. Ghost-talk
        is all the rage
in this blood-stained land, a boon
        for sisters, mothers

muzzled by recent griefs; but
        there is another source
of salvation Harriet has come
        to seek—some glimpse

beyond life's dark passage,
        some sisterhood
of "hand stretched forth
        to meet kindred hand"...

Charlotte's not in heaven;
        but from its antechamber
she expresses calm, "the frailties
        of life passing away." There are

other secrets to confide—Emily's
        skulking by the fire, storm
petrels looping by the tide; a husband's gentle
        hands...In the gloaming

ravens launch to roosts; the pencil
        comes to pause.
What's to doubt of this hereafter or that
        Charlotte speaks

when her complaints
        against carping critics
pierce the dazzle
        of a tranquil afterlife?

Rogue Dream for Emily Brontë

Staffordshire, England, 1994

I'm back in that borrowed house in the Peak District,
scribbling away from six-to-six, an intrepid
hiker not yet fazed by the discomforts of pregnancy.
Evenings, I entertain a husband's colleagues,
spin clouds of flour into cake, let arguments
recede. Voices crackle from the spines
of tattered paperbacks propped along a shining
bedroom shelf, the homeowner's abandoned texts
from university flashing like omens of success. Somewhere
snow hares lope beyond the falcon's eye, dreamed of
and elusive prey. What terrifies me

about this world? Not its natural cruelty, as Emily
might say, thinking of her father's tales: factory workers
up in arms, looms smashed and lit with flame
in Luddite revolts. Standing in the hallway, moonlight
sluicing stone, the Emily I imagine lives on to old age,
studies wildlife and botany, becomes cartographer
and celebrated authoress who campaigns
for land preservation, women's rights. She travels
to a healing forest, stocks a cabinet
of wonders, returning from another kingdom
where she and her sisters thrive:
Charlotte long married with a raucous brood, Anne
an admired directrix of a girl's seminary—the vibrant
queens of fortune they composed themselves to be—
mothered by the floral-bounded, feral earth,
mothers of imagination, mistresses of mirth.

Crow Hill Postscript

> *Moments so dark as these I have never known—*
> —Charlotte Brontë, to Ellen Nussey, December 19, 1848,
> in a letter written several hours before Emily's death

> *I could hardly let Emily go—I wanted to hold her back then—and I want her back now—*
> —Charlotte Brontë, letter to William Smith Williams, June 4, 1849

My sister did not, even in her leaving, idle—
she walked swiftly out of time.
September seized and stunned
her with unexpected coughing fits; she stumbled
through days and chores, feeding pets and stoking fires
until she could no longer stand. By December
she was gone. For weeks her dog howled
outside her open bedroom door, Keeper
looking expectantly when I returned from town.
Each time I try to walk the trail toward
Crow Hill, I hear her call me on—
a voice as clear as if she ambled a few steps
ahead, staking out the music of a line. Who else
could marshal birds of prey and pace the stream's
scribbled frost? She practiced fevered fugues
and drew the stunted fir, learned to read
shifts of light that spelled the early signs of spring.
For her, labor was liberty, scouring carpets, kneading dough—
the flour a filmy curtain cast in early morning light.
                    Evenings, we argued:
which statesmen, poets would outlast time? Would
our Queen one day reverse her opinions on womens' roles?
Ghostly sounds are what's left to me—her laugh and clatter
in the kitchen, Tiger teasing at her heels.

My atlas holds her impish marginalia. *What is*,
she scrawled, *the word used to express
the enlitenment of a room?*

Who's Who in Brontëworld

Emily Brontë (1818-1848)

Poet and novelist; author of *Wuthering Heights*; lover of animals and wild landscapes. Emily was also a talented pianist and proficient artist. She and siblings Charlotte, Anne, and Branwell were still small children when their mother Maria died in 1821; the youngest, Anne, was only twenty months old. Their father, Anglican curate Patrick Brontë, never remarried.

Charlotte Brontë (1816-1855)

Longest-lived Brontë sibling and author of the novels *Jane Eyre, Villette, Shirley,* and *The Professor.* She curated the literary legacy of sisters Emily and Anne, at times revising their work to fit her own vision. Charlotte achieved literary stardom after Emily's death and married happily, but her life was cut short when she died in the early months of pregnancy.

Branwell Brontë (1817-1848)

Only son of Maria and Patrick Brontë. Despite early promise as a writer and painter, Branwell was employed only intermittently. The position he held longest was as a tutor, but he was fired after falling in love with his employer's wife. Branwell's opium and alcohol addictions strained the Brontë household. He died of tuberculosis. At his funeral, Emily caught the cold that led to her final illness.

Anne Brontë (1820-1849)

Author of the novels *Agnes Grey* and *The Tenant of Wildfell Hall.* Though often viewed as quiet and religious, Anne's heroines reflect her fierce resistance to law and society's restrictions on women. Like Branwell and Emily, Anne contracted tuberculosis in 1848 and spent her last days in Scarborough with Charlotte, enjoying the seascape she loved.

Elizabeth Branwell/Aunt Branwell (1776-1842)

Relatively well-to-do sister of Maria Brontë, she arrived at Haworth in 1821 to help care for the Brontë children during their mother's decline. She ended up staying for the rest of her life, providing a guiding presence, overseeing their education, and assisting financially.

Emily's companions

Keeper, a mastiff; Nero, an injured hawk rescued from the moors; Tiger, a tabby; Adelaide and Victoria, a pair of geese. In a diary paper dated July 30, 1845, Emily notes the hawk and geese went "missing" during the time she and Charlotte spent studying in Belgium.

Ellis Bell, Currer Bell, Acton Bell

Aware of the literary culture's hostility toward women writers, the sisters chose pseudonyms for their joint poetry volume, *Poems by Currer, Ellis, and Acton Bell* (1846) and for publishing the novels that appeared during their lifetimes.

§

Haworth and Haworth Parsonage

Haworth Parsonage was the Brontë family's home and is now the Brontë Parsonage Museum. The Parsonage sits next to St. Michael and All Angels Church; the alley behind the house offers views of the moors along paths the sisters would have walked.

During the Brontë family's lifetime, Haworth was in the midst of rapid industrialization. Mortality was high, and villagers made their living through subsistence farming or soon-to-be obsolete domestic enterprises such as hand-loom weaving. Nearby, the open space of the moors with its crags, meadows, marshes, and harsh tumultuous winds fueled Emily's imagination.

About the Brontës

Despite limited formal schooling and lifetimes mostly spent in an isolated parsonage in Haworth village, Yorkshire, the Brontë sisters—Emily, Charlotte, and Anne—were well educated and highly attentive to the history and politics of their era. From their father Patrick, who held the modestly paid position of perpetual curate of Haworth, they inherited literary ambition and a love of learning. A widower, he allowed his children, including son Branwell, to range widely among his books, and they borrowed others from the nearby Heaton family's extensive library at Ponden Hall, later the inspiration for key locations in the sisters' novels.

Their mother (néeMaria Branwell) had died when Emily was three, and the lives of the two eldest sisters, Maria and Elizabeth, ended at ages ten and eleven (they contracted tuberculosis during their brief residency in boarding school). Understandably, the remaining siblings (Charlotte, Branwell, Emily, and Anne) forged close bonds with each other. In adult life, they ventured beyond the familiar realm of their childhood home through posts as tutors, governesses, and teachers.

From February-November 1842, Emily and Charlotte studied French in Belgium in hopes of eventually gaining financial independence by opening a school of their own in the Haworth parsonage. (The sisters' travel abroad was financed by their Aunt Branwell, their mother's sister, who moved to Haworth during her sister's illness and remained to care for Patrick's motherless brood.) The school plan didn't work out—no one enrolled—and, sadly, Aunt Branwell died during their excursion.

Their brother Branwell's literary promise was compromised by addiction and illness (he'd hoped to become a noted poet and did manage to publish alongside reputable authors in respected journals). Instead, it was Emily, Charlotte, and Anne who ended up producing the novels that reflected both a strong resistance to the era's social conventions and secured the sisters' lasting reputations. In order to do so, however, the trio had to break into print as men, adopting the pseudonyms of Currer, Ellis, and Acton Bell, three literary brothers, in order to both protect their privacy and ensure that their work would be taken seriously.

§

Letter to Emily Brontë: Italicized language is Charlotte's, from *Jane Eyre*. Other poems in dialogue with the sisters' work where italics appear include **Own the Charlotte Brontë, Volumes, Forfeit,** and **Rewriting Emily.** Among sources I returned to in writing these and other poems: *Wuthering Heights*, Emily and Anne's diary papers, Charlotte's letters and introduction to revised editions of her sisters' novels, Charlotte's novel *Shirley*, Anne's preface to *The Tenant of Wildfell Hall*.

Becoming a Brontë: Possible reasons for Patrick Brontë's choice include an association with the Greek world "bronte" (meaning thunder) and a fascination with the Royal Navy's Admiral Nelson, who received the honorary title "Duke of Bronté" from the King of Two Sicilies.

"Made Alive in the Usual Manner": Pillar Portrait of the Brontë Sisters, ca. 1834: Envisioning a career as a portrait artist, Branwell Brontë painted his three sisters and himself as a group; at some point later, his image was painted over to form a pillar, leaving only his sisters visible. The siblings' juvenilia formed an elaborate paracosm; a favored plot device was resurrecting villains and heroes.

Hunger Strike, Haworth, Yorkshire, ca. 1836: The poem reimagines an incident noted on the Brontë Parsonage Museum website: "In December 1836 Tabby slipped on ice in Haworth's main street, badly breaking her leg. Aunt Branwell suggested she leave the Parsonage to be nursed by her sister Susannah, but the children objected, even going on hunger strike, and Tabby stayed in the Parsonage, nursed by the children. The leg never fully healed, however, and over the next three years many of Tabby's duties were taken up by Emily."

Self-Portrait as Thunder and Lightning: The epigraph quotes Chloe Pirrie, who plays Emily in a production of Sally Wainwright's PBS Masterpiece Series drama, *To Walk Invisible: The Brontë Sisters.* Italics in line 14 are from advice given by Robert Southey, the Poet Laureate, to Charlotte Brontë, Keswick, March 1837 (Juliet Barker, *The Brontës: A Life in Letters*). Charlotte wrote Southey requesting literary advice; she was twenty-one at the time.

Emily's Apocrypha: Companions of Emily here include the merlin Nero and the mastiff Keeper. I've borrowed the phrase "a devouring flame" from Charlotte's description of her sister's fiercely loyal pet.

Animalia: Along with Nero the hawk, Emily refers to her geese Adelaide and Victoria.

The Badass Brontës: The siblings' father kept a pistol for self-defense and taught Emily to shoot. (In a town where domestic weaving was being displaced by a growing textile industry, the memory of Luddite rebellions against factory technology was still fresh.)

The Brothers Bell Plead Publishers Not to be Unmasked: William Smith Williams, a partner in the publishing firm Smith, Elder, & Co., became Charlotte's literary confidante. The poem adapts some of her comments regarding the reading public's queries about the sisters' true identities.

Emily, Inked: Van Diemen's Land (a British colony in Tasmania) housed convicts in its penal colonies. *Gondal* is the imaginary kingdom Emily and Anne invented as children; both sisters' early poems were inspired by Gondal settings and characters.

Who is Heathcliff? and **Heathcliff's Curse**: italicized lines are Emily's, borrowed from *Wuthering Heights.*

Haworth of Other Days: The title and opening line echo Donald Justice's "Miami of Other Days." Virginia Woolf's visit to the Brontë homestead is vividly captured in "Haworth, 1904," her first published essay. Today, the Black Bull tavern frequented by Branwell is a working pub and popular Haworth tourist spot.

Night: In a July, 1845 letter addressed to Ellen Nussey, Charlotte's account of her brother's "illnesses" (i.e., addictions) casts further light on the sisters' post-childhood family life: "I found Branwell ill—he is so very often owing to his own fault—...no one in the house could have rest—...he has written to me this morning and...promises amendment on his return—but so long as he remains at home I scarce dare hope for peace in the house—..." (Juliet Barker, *The Brontës: A Life in Letters*).

The Consequences of Desire/Brontë Bodies: A speculative sequence about pregnancy, contraception, and abortion in the Brontë's time. Written in the aftermath of the U.S. Supreme Court's Dobbs decision.

The poem draws on Anne's preface to the second edition of *The Tenant of Wildfell Hall* and Charlotte's letter to her friend, Amelia Taylor. Claire Harman's *Charlotte Brontë: A Fiery Heart* provides another compelling detail: after learning of Charlotte's death, novelist Elizabeth Gaskell—a sister in the arts and author of the first Brontë biography—confided in a letter to Catherine Winkworth her belief she could have "induced" Charlotte to do what was needed to save her life.

Archival: "*[A]n exhortation of course: courage!*" is borrowed from Emily Brontë's diary paper, July 30, 1841.

Sestina for Hiraeth, with Titles of Plath Poems from Early 1963: *Hiraeth* is a Welsh word of ancient lineage with no precise English equivalent that captures a feeling of impossible longing for a time, place, or homeland that may exist more powerfully in memory than in reality.

"These held the power to scatter Belgium's mist": In 1842, Charlotte and Emily Brontë were pupils in the Pensionnat Heger in Brussels, where they hoped to master French in preparation for opening a school for girls at the Parsonage (their plan never got off the ground).

Sylvia Plath visited the Brontë Parsonage Museum on September 28, 1956, during a post-honeymoon visit to Ted Hughes' family in Yorkshire.

Charlotte Brontë: The Séance: Inspired by accounts in Emily Midorikawa and Emma Claire Sweeney's *A Secret Sisterhood: The Literary Friendships of Jane Austen, Charlotte Bronte, George Eliot and Virginia Woolf* and Marlene Springer's *Biography* article "Stowe and Eliot: An Epistolary Friendship." Sophie Franklin's *Charlotte Bronte, Revisited* offered helpful insights about Charlotte's contemporaries. Line 24 quotes Thackeray's words about Charlotte, in an 1853 letter to Lucy Baxter; lines 43-44 and 47-48 are drawn from Harriet Beecher Stowe's letter to George Eliot, May 25, 1869.

Rogue Dream for Emily Brontë: Emily and Anne Brontë died of tuberculosis at age thirty and twenty-nine, respectively. Charlotte, who married curate Arthur Bell Nicholls, survived until the age of thirty-eight but died early in pregnancy due to severe morning sickness (hyperemesis gravidarum).

Crow Hill Postscript: Ellen Nussey was Charlotte's former school friend, lifelong correspondent, and a frequent visitor to the Parsonage during the sisters' lifetime.

Acknowledgements

Thanks are due to the editors of publications in which the following poems first appeared or are forthcoming.

Beloit Poetry Journal: *Charlotte Brontë: The Séance*

Burrow Press Review Nature Issue: *Gigan for a Pandemic Winter*

The Common: *Letter to Emily Brontë*

The Hopkins Review: *Reading Emily Brontë by Long Island Sound; The Badass Brontës; Emily's Apocrypha*

Interim: *Emily Brontë's Advice for the Anthropocene; Spellcasters; Errant Queen*

Literary Matters: *Night; Which Brontë Sister Are You?; Discarded Books at Flood Tide; Haworth of Other Days*

Missouri Review: *Self-Portrait as Thunder and Lightning; Costumery: Cento with Lines from Early Reviews of* Wuthering Heights; *Rewriting Emily; Heathcliff's Curse*

Mezzo Cammin: *Autobiographia Literaria; The Most* Wuthering Heights *Day Ever; Crow Hill Postscript*

Ocean State Review: *Emily, Inked*

Orion: *The Sharp-Shinned Hawk*

Plath Profiles: *Sestina for Hiraeth, with Titles of Plath Poems from Early 1963*

Plume: *Volumes*

Shenandoah: *Animalia; Errand Hanging with Emily Brontë*

"Forfeit" was awarded the 2015 Ledbury Festival Poetry Prize and appeared in *Hwaet! Twenty Years of the Ledbury Poetry Festival* (Bloodaxe, 2016), edited by Mark Fisher.

§

I'm deeply grateful to New York Public Library for access to Brontë materials in the Berg Collection and to Lyndsi Barnes and Joshua McKeon for their patience and assistance. During the pandemic, the programming resources provided by The Brontë Society and Brontë Parsonage Museum offered a rich source of inspiration.

Among biographical sources I found invaluable: Juliet Barker's *The Brontës: Wild Genius on the Moors: The Story of a Literary Family* (St. Martin's, 1994) and *The Brontës: A Life in Letters* (Overlook, 2002); Lucasta Miller's

The Brontë Myth (Knopf, 2003); Stevie Davies' *Emily Brontë: Heretic* (The Women's Press Ltd., 1994); Deborah Lutz's *The Brontë Cabinet* (W.W. Norton, 2015), and Adelle Hay's *Anne Brontë Reimagined* (Saraband, 2020).

Thanks are due to the Vermont Studio Center and Virginia Center for the Creative Arts for residencies that provided tranquility and community for the completion of this project. In addition, Loyola University Maryland provided welcome support in the form of travel funds and summer research grants.

I'm indebted to Nicole Cooley, Dana Curtis, Rachel Hadas, Andrew Hudgins, Mark Jarman, John Matthias, Paisley Rekdal, David St. John, Dan Tobin, Lesley Wheeler, and David Yezzi for spending time with these poems and offering generous support. Gratitude, also, to longtime colleagues Kathy Forni and Mark Osteen for cheering me on.

Among this project's earliest supporters are two gifted friends no longer with us: Kim Bridgford and Jon Tribble whose memory I value and whose words continue to inspire.

Shout outs to Camille Dungy, Shara McCallum, Penelope Pelizzon—sisters in poetry—for hours at The Blue Chair Café and beyond. Thanks to fellow writers at the West Chester University and Poetry by the Sea Global Conferences for companionship along the way.

Thanks to Zoë Shankle Donald, Patty Paine, Law Alsobrook, and everyone at Diode Editions for their care and support.

Ned Balbo, purveyor of Brontë-inspired music and other magic, went on long walks, bought me first editions, joined me in watching Brontë adaptations, read and re-read these poems. Reader, I'm a lucky writer to have married him.

Jane Satterfield's six books of poetry include *The Badass Brontës* (a Diode Editions winner, 2023) and *Apocalypse* Mix (2017, Autumn House Poetry Prize). She is also the author of *Her Familiars* (Elixir Press, 2013), *Assignation at Vanishing Point* (Elixir Press Book Award, 2003), and *Shepherdess with an Automatic* (WWPH, 2000, Towson University Prize for Literature). Sections from Satterfield's *Daughters of Empire: A Memoir of a Year in Britain and Beyond* (Demeter Press, 2009) received Florida Review's Editors' Prize, the Faulkner Society/Pirate's Alley Essay Award, and the John Guyon Literary Nonfiction Prize. With Laurie Kruk, she co-edited the multi-genre anthology *Borderlands and Crossroads: Writing the Motherland*.

Satterfield received a National Endowment for the Arts poetry fellowship and several Maryland State Arts Council awards. Individual poems have won *Bellingham Review's* 49th Parallel Poetry Prize, as well as the Ledbury Festival Poetry Prize and the *Mslexia* women's poetry prize (both U.K. awards). She has been a Walter E. Dakin fellow at the Sewanee Writers' Conference and received residency fellowships from the Arvon Foundation (U.K.), the Vermont Studio Center, the Virginia Center for the Creative Arts, and the Bread Loaf Writers' Conference.

Satterfield's poetry, prose, and lyric essays have appeared in *American Poetry Review, Antioch Review, The Common, Crazyhorse, DIAGRAM, Ecotone, Hotel Amerika, Hopkins Review, Missouri Review, North American Review, Notre Dame Review, Orion, Pleiades, Shenandoah,* and elsewhere, as well as on *Verse Daily* and *Poetry Daily*. She has served on the faculty of the West Chester Poetry Conference and as the 2019 Salisbury, Maryland Poet-in-Residence.

Satterfield is married to poet Ned Balbo. Born in Corby, England, to a British mother also born in Corby, she holds an MFA from the University of Iowa and is a professor of writing at Loyola University Maryland.